IMAGES OF ENGLAND

HARBORNE
THE SECOND SELECTION

IMAGES OF ENGLAND

HARBORNE
THE SECOND SELECTION

MARTIN HAMPSON

The
History
Press

High Street, *c.* 1910, showing a previous rebuilding of the King's Arms, with the spire of the old Baptist Chapel closing the view beyond.

Frontispiece: Harborne countryside, in winter. This is Church Farm Golf Course, in 1969.

First published 2002 by Tempus

Reprinted 2017 by

The History Press
The Mill, Brimscombe Port,
Stroud, Gloucestershire, GL5 2QG
www.thehistorypress.co.uk

British Library Cataloguing in Publication Data.
A catalogue record for this book is available from the British Library.

ISBN 978 0 7524 2658 7

Typesetting and origination by Tempus Publishing Limited.
Printed in Great Britain by TJ International Ltd, Padstow, Cornwall

Contents

Clent House, *c.* 1913, stood on the corner of St Peter's Road and Harborne Park Road.

Acknowledgements

I am grateful to Birmingham Library Services for allowing me to use their photographs. Special thanks are due to Harborne Library staff (particularly Mary Worrall and Wendy Carter) for making the Donald Wright Collection freely available, and to Mrs Betty Wright for help and advice, and for giving permission for me to make extensive use of her late husband's collection. The Harborne Collection features on pages 2, 4, 6, 13, 14a, 15, 16, 19b, 25b, 26b, 33a, 34b, 35b, 37a, 42, 43a, 44a, 47a, 48b, 49a, 51a, 52b, 53, 55a, 56a, 57, 58a, 59, 60, 64, 65a, 66, 68, 69, 70b, 72a, 73b, 74a, 75a, 76, 77, 81b, 83b, 87, 88b, 89, 90b, 91-4, 98a, 99, 100a, 101, 105, 107b, 108, 113a, 115, 116a, 118, 119, 121a, 122, 124, 126-128. I am further indebted to Mrs Betty Wright for the loan of 19a, 40a, 67, 82a, 106a. Thanks are also due to Mr and Mrs J. Waggett for their permission to use 62a and 125b; to Mr K. Sutton for 54b; to Mrs D. Sadler for 83b, 91b and 92a; to St Mary's School (Fiona Birt) for 84b, 85, 86 and 123; and the Moorpool Players for 110 and 111. I should also like to thank David Harvey for his help, Martin Flynn for encouragement in the early stages, and Local Studies staff for customary technical assistance. Finally, I am grateful to Roy Clarke, the author of the first Harborne volume, for setting a fine example in that work, and for offering encouragement and support for this sequel.

Introduction

A word of explanation is perhaps required for the appearance of the present volume. The previous selection of Harborne photographs – by my colleague, Roy Clarke – was justly popular, and it was felt that a second volume was justified, because some interesting photographs remained unused, and more had been added to the Library's collections since the appearance of the first book in 1994. I have tried to make this selection complementary to Roy Clarke's book, by including new images of subjects previously touched upon, as well as introducing fresh topics.

Harborne – one of Birmingham's ancient villages – appears in the Domesday Book of 1086 as 'Horeborne', there being land for only one plough let out to a certain 'Robert'. No church is mentioned, and the village would at this time be no more than a tiny hamlet, situated in a clearing with a spring of drinking water – probably the spring at present in the grounds of Harborne Hall, which feeds the spring in Grove Park.

Several explanations have been offered for the name 'Harborne', including 'muddy stream' and 'ancient boundary'. Either carries some conviction, the first on account of the number of streams, pools and natural springs in the area (sometimes coloured by the clay soil); the second because in Anglo-Saxon times the village marked the southernmost boundary of the Mercian diocese. While Bishop of Mercia (669-72), St Chad is said to have raised a boundary cross here.

Although documentary evidence for St Peter's church dates back only to 1217, what is believed to have been the base of St Chad's preaching cross was discovered during excavations beneath St Peter's in 1983, suggesting that an earlier church existed on the site. For much of its history, the Manor of Harborne remained church property, the right to appoint vicars being the prerogative of the Dean and Chapter of Lichfield (apart from a Reformation interlude), until it was transferred to the new Birmingham diocese in 1905.

For many centuries, Harborne remained a small Staffordshire farming community, whose income was, from the sixteenth century, supplemented by nail making. Clay-pit working and associated brick-works were later established. By the time of the 1801 census, the population was still only 1,178 and no more than 1,637 by 1841. The main settlement had by 1841 moved away from the church, and was clustered round the crossroads at the King's Arms (site of the original village green). Early ribbon development was gradually extending down the High Street, whose lower residential half was known as Heath Road. Another small settlement, known as Harborne Heath, occupied the area round the Green Man, at the Metchley Lane crossroads. There were, in addition, a number of large residences, stretching from near the church towards the High Street, which were occupied by local dignitaries.

Further growth was initially to the south of the High Street; but with the opening of the Harborne Railway in 1874 there was development to the north as well. The railway encouraged commuting into the city centre, so that businessmen and clerical workers came increasingly to settle here. Moreover, although Harborne developed some new industries of its own (such as the Chad Valley Toy Company), it remained predominantly a residential area, this trend being encouraged by the proximity of Edgbaston, a pioneering garden suburb already established by the mid-nineteenth century. Industrial ribbon development and high-density housing were specifically forbidden in Edgbaston, so that it came to serve as a green 'buffer zone' between Harborne and the city centre.

Local government in Harborne began with the setting up of the Local Board of Health in 1864, followed by a School Board in 1873. The village became part of Birmingham, thus leaving Staffordshire for Warwickshire, in 1891. The establishment of a public library in 1892 was one of the first benefits of this union. By 1901, the population had grown to 10,113. The first major housing development of the area occurred in this decade, with the establishment in 1908 of J.S. Nettlefold's Moorpool Estate. Reflecting the contemporary garden city movement in its green and spacious layout and the cottage style of its houses, the Moorpool enterprise was distinctive in its co-partnership principle, whereby tenants would take up shares in the managing company and eventually have a controlling interest in it. Like Bournville, it provided a model for future local and national developments, offering good quality housing at affordable rents, with a special emphasis on private gardens and public recreation grounds. The post war council estate of Metchley Grange clearly owes something to the Moorpool layout in its retention of many mature trees, its use of off-street housing reached by footpaths, and in the role of its own natural pool as a focal point.

Several factors combined early to fix Harborne's character as a semi-rural suburb still often referred to as a village. Harborne Golf Club was founded in 1893, soon afterwards developing former farmland on either side of Northfield Road into what ultimately became two courses, one private, one municipal. To this permanent open space was later added on the southern side the Woodgate Valley Country Park, preserved former farmland between Quinton and Bartley Green. East of the course, beyond St Peter's large wooded churchyard, Harborne Hall, with its extensive conservation garden, was retained for a variety of institutional uses. Across Grove Lane, the Grove Estate, given to the city in 1963, is still today a green oasis, remaining fundamentally unchanged forty years after the demolition of the house. The adjoining house and park became in 1911 the official residence of the Bishops of Birmingham, thus ensuring a further incentive for retaining the character of the area. Beyond Bishop's Croft, the spacious cricket grounds, traversed by the tree-lined Old Church Avenue, remain a popular facility, substantially unaltered over the past century.

Harborne is an important educational centre, being particularly notable for the quality of its junior schools (including Birmingham's oldest, St Peter's); and is the home of the long-established and innovative Queen Alexandra College for the Blind. Several nationally known people have lived here, including the poet W.H. Auden (whose childhood homes were on Lordswood Road and Court Oak Road) and the parliamentary reformer Thomas Attwood (who lived at The Grove). Abraham Lincoln's consular representative Elihu Burritt lived on Victoria Road while writing a pioneering investigative report on the Black Country. The painter David Cox lived on Greenfield Road.

In the last century, the name of Harborne was nationally known for several reasons. Children had reason to know it for the Chad Valley Toy Company, which flourished there for seventy-five years; and also perhaps as the place where the world's first Girl Guide troop was formed in 1909. Culturally, however, the most significant event occurred in 1963, when the Victoria and Albert Museum decided to transfer the panelled ante-room of The Grove (due to be demolished) for permanent preservation in their Victorian Primary Galleries. Now known as the Harborne Room, it fittingly commemorates the work of the Birmingham architect J.H. Chamberlain, whose richly ornate Victorian Gothic style still adorns several surviving houses in Harborne and Edgbaston, including Harborne Hall. Chamberlain designed The Grove for the Kenricks, who in themselves embodied Victorian Birmingham's two abiding concerns – manufacturing and the arts.

In spite of losing some of its older specialised family businesses, Harborne High Street remains an attractive focal point for a wide area, valued for catering facilities as well as shopping. The prevalence of a strong community spirit, characteristic of a village, is borne out by the number of surviving social, cultural and sporting associations, many of them of long standing. It has been an aim of this book to capture something of this still enduring character, in earlier and in more recent scenes.

One

Rural Scenes

A lone walker strolls up Ridgeacre Lane, *c.* 1913.

This view towards Harborne, from fields above Weoley Castle ruins, was taken in 1932. In the foreground can be seen Weoley Castle Farm, which stood where Alwold Road now runs, with the remains of Weoley Castle moat beyond. To the left is the lane, now reduced to a footpath, which runs up to Stonehouse Farm, seen among the trees on the left, with Stonehouse Hill and Northfield Road beyond. To the right, in the distance, may be seen the now demolished Weymoor Farm, beyond which lies today the Hillyfields Estate. All the intervening fields are now covered with Weoley Castle housing. This picture emphasises how rural was the whole area to the south and south west of Harborne, even as late as the early 1930s.

The footpath through the Hillyfields, seen here *c.* 1920, still survives today as a pedestrian thoroughfare, although the Hillyfields housing estate now occupies the land to the right and Church Farm Golf Course the land to the left. Former farms in the area are commemorated in the names Weymoor Road and Mill Farm Road, and the nature of the farmland itself by Sedgehill Avenue, Kelfield Avenue and Ferncliffe Road.

Harts Green Farm, *c.* 1930, stood in the angle between Fellows Lane and Tennal Road, where the shopping centre at the foot of War Lane now stands. It remained a flourishing dairy farm, selling fresh milk, into the 1930s. Following its demolition in 1934 as part of the Harts Green Estate development, the poplar trees in its front garden survived, being only recently cut down.

These seventeenth-century cottages in Lordswood Road, *c*. 1960, are a reminder of the kind of traditional houses seen on or around Harborne High Street in fairly large numbers into quite recent times. Much of the High Street itself was originally residential, and many present-day shops are, in fact, older house conversions. These particular cottages, close to Frankley Terrace, were demolished in around 1980.

Lordswood Road, *c*. 1920, is seen here shortly before major housing developments. At this time, only the Harborne end of the road was developed, and it was there, first on Lordswood Road and then on nearby Court Oak Road, that the poet W.H. Auden lived in his youth, his father being Professor of Public Health at Birmingham University. Lordswood Road takes its name from the Lord's Wood, which stretched on the left-hand side up to Hagley Road.

St Mary's Road, c. 1907. Named after the nearby Catholic church, this road is noteworthy for having a number of large Victorian and Edwardian houses of the kind more frequently found in Edgbaston. In this view, the road remains partly undeveloped.

Vicarage Road, seen here in around 1933, is an ancient road originally leading to outlying parts of the parish. It is partly a 'holloway', the road already worn deep by the middle ages; a similar effect is seen in Fellows Lane, its continuation.

Old Church Avenue, as it is now called, crosses the cricket grounds, linking Harborne Park Road with Old Church Road and thus forming a direct link between the village and St Peter's church. Seen here, *c.* 1913, it is referred to in Elihu Burritt's 1868 account of the congregation of St Peter's coming, 'across the broad fields by footpaths that converge from every direction into the solemn aisles of the churchyard trees. The main avenue is nearly a third of a mile in length, with a lofty roofage half the way'.

The Verger's Cottage and St Peter's church, *c.* 1960, shortly before the cottage was demolished.

An aerial view of Bishop's Croft and its immediate setting, *c.* 1962, showing the 'green heart' of Harborne, which is now a conservation area. Originally a seventeenth-century mansion known as Harborne House, Bishop's Croft was rebuilt in around 1790 by Thomas Green, a nail-master, soon after he had purchased the manor of Harborne. It was bought by the Church Commissioners in 1911, following the creation of the new Birmingham diocese in 1905, as the official residence of the Bishops of Birmingham. The first resident was the second Bishop, Henry Russell Wakefield. The church commissioned a number of renovations in the Arts and Crafts style by A.S. Dixon, including a private chapel in the grounds, which can be seen at right angles to the house. Behind the house lie Harborne Cricket Club grounds, traversed by Old Church Avenue. To the left of the picture may be seen the Lodge to Bishop's Croft and beyond that St Peter's school. Just discernible in the bottom right-hand corner is Harborne Park Road, where the Diocesan Offices were built in 1965.

This view of St Peter's church, from the point where St Peter's Road joins Old Church Road, c. 1891, is scarcely recognisable today. A lychgate was shortly afterwards erected (in 1892) at this point to commemorate the life and work of Eliza Roberts, who had run the Vicarage school from 1853 to 1890. The cottage on the left became Harborne's first post office in 1844, when Samuel Dugmore, the district registrar, was also appointed postmaster. He served too as the village postman, and it was only after his retirement in 1862 that the post office was transferred to the High Street. The cottages on the right have all been demolished, the site being now occupied by modern housing. The view of the church itself is obscured today by lofty mature trees.

The entrance to Metchley Park Road in 1933, shortly before housing developments.

Cottages (now demolished) which stood in Metchley Lane, near the Green Man, *c.* 1930.

Harborne Lane, approaching Harborne from Selly Oak, in 1925. As late as the mid-1920s, the scene remained semi-rural, with fields and allotments, tall hedges and mature trees. In the middle distance may be seen the original Golden Cross pub, then serving the small community of Victorian terraces at the junction of Harborne Lane and Metchley Lane. The foreground of this scene is now partly occupied by pre-war semis, while a 1960s housing estate covers the site of the allotments and some of the fields beyond. The Queen Elizabeth Hospital now occupies a site to the far right of the picture.

The Moor Pool, seen here in the 1970s, is fed by a natural spring. Originally, it would be used by the villagers for bathing, drinking and washing purposes; in the nineteenth century taking in washing was a common activity for local women. Now forming an attractive focal point for the Moorpool Estate (which, like Bournville, retained many natural features, including mature trees and woodland), it is much frequented by fishermen, and also provides a harmonious backdrop for the Moorpool Bowling Club, whose pavilion may be seen on the right.

Tennal Road, c. 1906, with country cottages sheltering behind tall hedges.

Watching cows grazing off Ridgeacre Lane in the 1920s.

At the point of change. Trees being felled in Tom Knocker's Wood, preparatory to road and house building, in 1945. This site corresponds approximately to the present-day junction of Quinton Road and West Boulevard.

Two

Street Scenes

The junction of High Street and Vivian Road, *c.* 1905, with a horse-trough behind the lamp and a horse bus from Birmingham approaching on the right.

Harborne Lane, approaching the Bourn Brook bridge, in 1924, with Harborne Mill on the left and the Golden Cross straight ahead, behind the trees. A mill was first mentioned on this site in 1554. Involved in metalworking for much of its history, the mill, although now demolished, is remembered in the name of Water Mill Primary school.

Harborne Park Road in 1922, shortly before conversion to a dual carriageway. This was an ancient country lane, partly a 'holloway', as can be seen from the bank on the left.

Roadworks on Harborne Park Road in 1924.

Further roadworks on Harborne Park Road in 1924, showing incursions into The Grove estate on the right, with a number of mature trees already being felled to make way for the central reservation. On the journey to Selly Oak, the original country road now forms the left-hand traffic lane.

Harborne Park Road in 1926, with the roadworks now completed in readiness for the new No.11 (Outer Circle) bus route. The old entrance lodge to The Grove originally stood opposite the Mock Tudor house on the left; demolished for the central reservation, it has been replaced by the lodge on the right. New fencing can be seen, marking the pushed-back boundaries of The Grove estate.

Harborne Park Road, a little further down the hill, looking in the opposite direction, towards central Harborne, in the 1970s. Grove Park, on the left, now an open-plan public park at this point, had been given to the city in 1963.

The junction of Harborne Park Road and Metchley Lane in 1924, showing the original Golden Cross pub; apart from this and the buildings on the far right, most of the houses in the picture have survived. To the right, there is now a small council estate.

Harborne Park Road in 1961, near the junction with the High Street. The terraces beyond the tall gabled house have all been demolished; the new Baptist church now occupies the site between the trees.

The junction of Northfield Road and Tennal Road in 1935, with Harts Green Farm already demolished in readiness for the new estate development. At this time, some farmworkers' cottages still survived on the left, and the poplars were to remain until quite recently as a reminder of the original rural scene.

The junction of War Lane and Victoria Road in 1909.

Fellows Lane in 1938, before road widening.

Tennal Road in 1935, still partly a country lane, with the bank of a 'holloway' on the left.

The junction of Court Oak Road and Croftdown Road in the 1960s, with St Faith and St Lawrence church on the left, the Court Oak pub on the right, and Queen's Park straight ahead.

Lordswood Road in 1930, showing substantial housing developments from the 1920s. Like Harborne Park Road, this road was upgraded to accommodate the new Outer Circle bus route. Although the Harborne end was built up by the Edwardian period, Lordswood Road's most characteristic phase saw the erection of a number of large detached houses in the inter-war period. There have been further developments, including flats and semis, since the war.

A tram approaching its terminus by the King's Head on Hagley Road in the 1920s, with Lordswood Road running off to the right. The Bearwood / Harborne boundary runs just before the pub. There was already a small housing settlement in this area by the 1830s.

Harborne Terrace, at the junction of Harborne High Street and Lordswood Road, in 1922, with a small family business liberally endowed with miscellaneous advertisements. This terrace, of seventeenth-century origin, is characteristic of other older properties on the High Street, which were originally houses and have been converted into shops. In the picture, mixed use is apparent, with some houses still private residences, and a passage leading to a court of dwellings behind. Part of this terrace survives, still partly residential.

The pub was rebuilt between the wars, and destroyed by fire in 2013. The site currently awaits a new use.

Looking down the High Street in the late 1930s, with the recently reconstructed King's Arms on the right and part of Harborne Terrace on the left.

Looking in the opposite direction, towards Prince's Corner and War Lane, again in the 1930s. This marks the site of the original village green.

A view up Albert Walk, towards the King's Arms, in the 1980s. The garden centre on the left was for some years a popular attraction. Albert Walk was at one time the starting point for a field path to St Peter's church. The buildings on the left form part of Prince's Corner, also named after Prince Albert.

The Junction Inn and High Street, c. 1905, with Harborne Library (marked by two dormers) on the right. The Junction was built in 'gin palace' style by Wood and Kendrick in 1904, on the site of an earlier pub. Making distinctive use of its wedge-shaped corner position, it is richly decorated in terracotta. The horse-trough shown in front of the pub was for many years a popular meeting place. Beyond the Library can be seen some terraced housing which still survives, again emphasising the continual mix of residential and commercial use on the High Street.

Looking down the High Street from the Junction, *c.* 1905.

The High Street decorated for the Coronation of George V in 1911.

Modern shop fronts on the High Street conceal former eighteenth-century houses, 1975.

The lower end of the High Street, looking towards Birmingham, *c.* 1912, with the Board school (now the School Yard restaurant and residential complex) overlooking an incoming horse bus.

The lower end of High Street, looking in the opposite direction, towards the original Junction pub, c. 1903. The front garden of a large private house – one of several then at this point – can be seen on the right.

Old houses on the High Street, now demolished, seen here in 1963.

Greenfield Road in the 1980s. Now a conservation area, this is one of Harborne's most distinct-ive roads, containing a wide variety of housing, ranging from large ornate terraces to simple cottages.

Renovated cottages in Greenfield Road in the 1980s.

South Street, seen here *c.* 1920, is one of three residential streets to the south of the High Street, erected by the Coleshill builder Josiah Bull York. South Street was originally Josiah Street, and the others are York Street and Bull Street. All three streets contain cottage-style terraced houses with small front gardens; some houses have Georgian-style frontages. To the left of this picture, marked by its spire, is Harborne Methodist church.

Another view of South Street, still substantially unchanged in the 1980s.

Looking down York Street in the early 1960s, with the White Horse on the right, adjacent to the Board school and the junction with the High Street. The White Horse is a typical nineteenth-century cottage-style pub, not dissimilar from its neighbours apart from the bay windows. The pub survives, recently revamped in 'alehouse' style, but the houses have gone.

Clarence Road, seen in the 1980s, is typical of several terraced streets to be found to the north of the High Street. Part of Harborne's late Victorian expansion, they were developed in stages, in small separately designed blocks rather than in a single monotonous style.

The Fish Inn, a prominent Harborne pub in the nineteenth and early twentieth centuries, stood just off the High Street, at the junction of North Road and Grays Road. It is seen here in around 1960, not long before its demolition. This part of Harborne was known originally as Harborne Heath, and at the time of the photograph was still densely built up with eighteenth and nineteenth century terraced housing, including a number of former nail-makers' cottages. Some of the latter still survive, but part of the area has been redeveloped, and an open space created between Nursery Road and Park Hill Road.

Moorpool Avenue, c. 1908, shortly after completion. This was a principal thoroughfare of the Harborne Tenants' (or Moorpool) Estate, designed by Frederick Martin for J.S. Nettlefold, and run on the co-partnership principle, whereby tenants could take up shares in the company and eventually acquire a controlling interest in it.

A recent view of Moorpool Avenue, showing an 'elephant crossing' road sign, which mysteriously appeared overnight in April 2000.

The Circle, Moorpool Estate, c. 1909, showing the community hall to the right of the shops. Unlike the near-contemporary garden suburb of Bournville, the Moorpool Estate never had a full-scale shopping centre of its own, owing to the nearness of Harborne High Street. It shared with Bournville, however, a green and spacious layout and a cottage style of housing.

Three

Houses and Housing

Houses in North Road due for demolition, *c.* 1960.

Harborne Hall from the meadows, c. 1921. Built by Thomas Green, a nail-master, around 1790 on the site of an earlier house, it passed to his nephew Thomas Green Simcox in 1813. The Simcoxes were associated with the house for some years, and the Harts from 1868 to 1883. Charles Joseph Hart, the director of an art metalwork company, was well known as a volunteer officer with the Royal Warwickshire Regiment and as founder of Harborne's original Fire Brigade. His successor, Walter Chamberlain (brother of Joseph), employed the architects Martin and Chamberlain to enlarge and Gothicise the original Georgian house. Walter Chamberlains's sister Mary married William Kenrick, who rebuilt the neighbouring Grove House, employing the same architects. The Chamberlains kept on the hall after they ceased to live there; it was used for Avery's staff recreation (Walter Chamberlain being a director of Avery's), and subsequently for the accommodation of Belgian refugees and as a military hospital. Following a short period as a preparatory school (1919-24), it subsequently became a convent and retreat house (1925-88), and has more recently served as a multi-faith centre, a VSO training centre and a hotel. Its extensive wooded grounds with a natural lake form a noted conservation garden.

The reception hall at Harborne Hall, *c.* 1921. This ornate galleried room was designed by Martin and Chamberlain as part of their rebuilding of the house in 1884, and recalls the very similar reception hall at Highbury, in Moseley, which they had built earlier for Joseph Chamberlain.

Charles Joseph Hart (1851-1925), as director of an art metalwork firm, personified the city's concerns with the arts and industry. He was also keenly interested in archaeology and architecture, and served for many years on the committee of the School of Art. He worked as Recruiting Officer for Birmingham during the First World War, enlisting over 80,000 men; but his best-known achievement today is probably the founding of Harborne Volunteer Fire Brigade in 1879; this was ultimately absorbed into the Birmingham fire service when Harborne was united with Birmingham in 1891.

Belgian refugees at Harborne Hall, *c.* 1915.

Elihu Burritt's house, Victoria Road, *c.* 1960. Elihu Burritt was appointed American consul to Birmingham by Abraham Lincoln; his purpose was to report on the industrial output, character and natural resources of the area. During his term of office (1865-9), he wrote an early tourist guide, *Walks in the Black Country and its green borderland* (1868), still considered one of the best books on the area. In this book, he admired much of what he saw; but was angered by child labour, long hours and low pay. He was actively involved in the local affairs of Harborne, and was a member of the committee responsible for the rebuilding of St Peter's church. His house still survives, now known as 'Burritt's House'.

The Grove, seen here in the 1930s, was originally a farmhouse, which was remodelled and extended in the late eighteenth century. In the early nineteenth century, it was the home of Thomas Attwood, who married Elizabeth Carless, daughter of the owner, and became famous as a parliamentary reformer and one of Birmingham's first two M.P's. In 1876, the house was acquired by William Kenrick, who the following year became Mayor of Birmingham, and later represented the city in Parliament. He commissioned the Ruskinian architect John Henry Chamberlain to rebuild the house in the Gothic style, retaining the foundations and some of the internal walls, but totally reconstructing the outer walls in local red brick with stone and terracotta dressings. An iron-founder by trade, William Kenrick also shared Chamberlain's artistic tastes, filling his house with Pre-Raphaelite paintings and Chinese pottery, in harmony with the architect's own ornate carving, gilding and marquetry. Closely linked with The Grove in his youth was the actor Alan Napier, whose mother was a Kenrick, and who played Batman's butler in the television series. The Grove estate was left to the City Council, who kept the park; but the house was pulled down in 1963. The richly panelled ante-room was dismantled and re-erected at the Victoria and Albert Museum, where it is known as the Harborne Room.

Thomas Attwood (1783-1856) was born in Halesowen; but came to Birmingham to work in his father's bank, moving to Harborne when he married Elizabeth Carless of The Grove. A dedicated parliamentary reformer, committed to peaceful progress at a time of civil unrest, he founded the Birmingham Political Union in 1830, determined to secure parliamentary representation for the city. The great Newhall Hill meeting of 10 May 1832, addressed by Attwood, led directly to the successful passage of the Reform Bill and Attwood's own election as one of Birmingham's first two MPs.

William Kenrick (1831-1919) originally wished to be an artist; but chose instead to enter the family firm, Archibald Kenrick & Sons, iron-founders and hollow-ware manufacturers. He married Mary Chamberlain, sister of Joseph Chamberlain, whose first wife was William Kenrick's sister. William Kenrick, like Joseph Chamberlain, came from a staunch liberal and nonconformist family. Each man chose the same architect (John Henry Chamberlain) to design his house; and each became Mayor of Birmingham and later MP for the city. William Kenrick was chairman of the School of Art Committee and a major patron of the Museum and Art Gallery. A personal friend of Burne-Jones, he filled The Grove with works by the leading painters of his day, the interior and furnishings still reflecting his artistic tastes at the time of the demolition of the house in 1963.

Mr J.H. Webb, head gardener at The Grove, holding his son Harry (who later founded the famous youth club, the Stonehouse Gang), is seen here in 1909.

Grove Park in 1966, looking towards Grove Lane, and showing the site of the then recently demolished house.

Church View, which stood on the corner of St Peter's Road and Old Church Road, is seen here in around 1930, with Harborne's former post office to the right of the picture. Formerly a pub (the Church Tavern), this attractive house has now been removed for road-widening, and modern flats occupy the site just behind.

St Peter's Vicarage, c. 1891, was built in the 1820s by the then vicar, James Thomas Law, and survived into the 1950s, when it was replaced by the present more manageable and modern building. It stood adjacent to the west door of the church; part of the boundary wall may still be seen in the car park, and a portion of the once extensive garden survives behind the parish hall.

Servants at St Peter's Vicarage, c. 1890.

Metchley Grange, c. 1890, the home of Sir Henry Wiggin, stood on the corner of Metchley Lane and what is now Malins Road. The Metchley Grange Housing Estate now occupies the site.

These flats on Metchley Lane are shown in 1965, shortly after their erection on the site of Metchley Grange.

Sir Henry Wiggin (1824-1905) and his wife Mary (nee Malins) have a substantial memorial in St Peter's church, which they attended regularly. The director of a large nickel smelting company, Sir Henry became Mayor of Birmingham and later MP for East Staffordshire and then Handsworth. He founded a group of almshouses, providing pensions for their occupants. A man of varied cultural, charitable and business interests, he was involved in the management of the Midland Railway, King Edward's school, the General Hospital, the University, the Blue Coat school, and the Joint Stock Bank, as well as helping found the Midland Institute.

Edward Capern's house, on Harborne High Street, in 1966, shortly before its demolition. Edward Capern (1819-94), a Bideford postman, moved to Harborne in 1868 to be near his son. While trudging the country lanes delivering his mail, he composed many of his poems. A friend of Elihu Burritt, he accompanied the consul on many of his walks, and wrote poetry that was said by the *Birmingham Post* to consist of 'delightful lyrics, as remarkable for their artlessness as for their beauty...among the best pastoral poems of the day'.

Sungleams and shadows (1881) was written by Edward Capern while he was living in Harborne. It contains several poems with a local theme – including *Harborne Churchyard*, *Lightwoods*, and *Frankley Beeches*. In 1884, owing to his wife's illness, Capern returned to Devon, dying in retirement there ten years later. Today he is remembered in the street name Capern Grove.

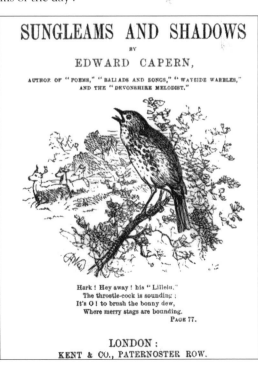

SUNGLEAMS AND SHADOWS

BY

EDWARD CAPERN,

AUTHOR OF "POEMS," "BALLADS AND SONGS," "WAYSIDE WARBLES," AND THE "DEVONSHIRE MELODIST."

Hark ! Hey away ! his "Lillelu."
The throstle-cock is sounding ;
It's O ! to brush the bonny dew,
Where merry stags are bounding.
PAGE 77.

LONDON :
KENT & CO., PATERNOSTER ROW.

Harborne, at one time, had a number of houses tucked away off the main streets, up secluded paths and drives. Some still survive; but post war redevelopment has cleared away many, including these cottages at the rear of Bull Street, seen in around 1960.

Frankley Terrace, off Lordswood Road, is so called because it commands an open view of Frankley Beeches. It is one of the few of Harborne's off-street terraces which have survived virtually intact, and many of the houses have now been fully restored. This view of *c.* 1960 shows an old cottage flanking the entrance to the terrace on the left.

A personalised Christmas card, sent in 1910 by Dr and Mrs Rowland Winn, of No 8 Albert Road, shows Mrs Winn standing in their wintry garden, with the house rising in the background.

Clent House, c. 1955, shortly before demolition. It stood at the junction of St Peter's Road and Harborne Park Road. Only the gateposts and garden wall now remain.

John Sutton Nettlefold (1866-1930) was a screw manufacturer whose family firm ultimately became GKN. The Unitarian families of Nettlefold and Chamberlain were already inter-related through marriage when John Nettlefold married a distant cousin, Margaret Chamberlain; the links were further strengthened by Joseph Chamberlains' having been for some time a partner in the family firm. The Nettlefolds were linked with other business and political families, including the Beales, Kenricks and Hopes. J.S. Nettlefold was an active local councillor, whose special interest in housing reform led to the creation of his most lasting achievement, the Harborne Tenants' (or Moorpool) Estate.

The first sod of the Moorpool Estate was cut by Mrs Nettlefold on 26 October 1907, and building operations began on 1 January 1908. Moorpool Avenue is seen here under construction later in the same year. Designed by Frederick Martin, the estate was to be run on the co-ownership principle, whereby tenants could buy shares in the company.

The Square, Moorpool Estate, *c.* 1922. Like George Cadbury's Bournville (which J.S. Nettlefold much admired), the estate was planned on 'green' principles, some woodland and mature trees being retained, and main roads following, where appropriate, the line of old country lanes (e.g., Moor Pool Lane becoming Ravenhurst Road). The natural lake, Moor Pool, was preserved as a focal point for the estate.

Moorpool Avenue, *c.* 1960. An emphasis was placed on wide tree-lined roads and sizeable gardens, at a time when much terraced housing was still being built without these. A community hall and adequate recreation grounds were provided, and allotments were available in addition to gardens for the especially enthusiastic.

East Pathway, Moorpool Estate, *c.* 1965. The houses varied considerably in size and form, from flats and cottage-style terraces to larger gabled semis.

Margaret Grove, Moorpool Estate, *c.* 1970. Built to forestall cheap speculative housing development, the estate made good use of the gently undulating site, as can be seen here, with the front gardens forming rockeries. At the time of foundation (1908), rents for the houses ranged between 4s 8d (23p) and 11s (55p) weekly. This road was named after the wife of the founder of the estate.

Tennal Hall, seen in 1910, stood close to the junction of the present-day Tennal Road and Tennal Lane. A Tudor manor house, believed to date from the fourteenth century, it had originally a massive front garden wall adorned by an intricately designed wrought iron gate.

A room in Tennal Hall, c. 1910. Farmed over the years by the Cave, Freeth and Pearman families, the house was said to have been visited by both Elizabeth I and the poet William Shenstone. It was demolished in 1937 to make way for a housing estate.

Wellington Lodge, also known as The Turrets, shortly before demolition in 1968. For long the home of the Cave-Browne-Cave family, it stood at the junction of Ravenhurst Road and Wentworth Road (itself known at one time as Wellington Road). The site is now occupied by modern flats.

Court Oak House, Court Oak Road, in 1974. Originally a private house, dating from the 1880s, it was bought by the City Council in 1906; they added the grounds to Queen's Park, and subsequently used it for a variety of official purposes. Ultimately becoming surplus to requirements, its condition seriously deteriorated in the 1970s, but it was eventually restored and successfully converted into flats.

Four

Work and Transport

Harborne Volunteer Fire Brigade, *c.* 1890.

Christmas preparations by Walter Mudd the fishmonger, at 133 Harborne High Street in 1904.

William Gardner, watchmaker and
jeweller, at 104 High Street, *c.* 1900.

George Tansley, fishmonger, at 158 High Street, c. 1908.

This shopping frontage, c. 1920, remains a recognisable feature of the High Street, although the occupants are all now different. The Crown Inn adjoins George Knowles the chemist, followed by Foster Bros. Clothing Co., then William Jones the draper. Foster Bros. had premises on Harborne High Street for virtually 100 years. The shop fronts with their balustraded tops are clearly later additions to what were formerly private houses with front gardens.

Shops and post office at The Circle, Moorpool Estate, in the late 1920s.

Woolley & Newey, grocer, at the junction of Victoria Road and Vicarage Road, c. 1912.

Shops on Grove Lane in 1960. These formed part of the Hillyfields Estate, built during the 1950s on the aptly named fields of that name which sloped down from Harborne Hall towards the Bourn Brook. The community hall was yet to be built at the far end of the shops.

INDOOR GAMES

DOMINOES G 59

LUDO G 37

DRAUGHTS AND BOARD G 108

LUDO G 103

BOARD GAMES
G 37 LUDO. Board and all components complete in box. Size 13½" x 6½" x 1".
G 38 SNAKES AND LADDERS. Details as for G 37.
G 97 SNAKES AND LADDERS. Separate board and box, plastic counters and dice box. Board size when open 14" x 14".
G 103 (5103) LUDO. Details as for G 97.

DRAUGHTS
G 42 DRAUGHTS BOARD. High quality folding board, covered in red, and with new label design. With cloth hinge, 14" x 14".
G 108 DRAUGHTSMEN AND BOARD. Twenty-four wooden men and new board with new box. Board 11½" x 11½". Box 12" x 7" x 1".
G 109 DRAUGHTSMEN. A set of twenty-four plastic interlocking men, black and red, 1½" diameter, in cardboard box.

CARD GAMES
Traditional games in pleasant presentations.
G 112 HAPPY FAMILIES.
G 113 SNAP.
G 114 OLD MAID.
G 115 CARTON. Assortment of two dozen packs.

DOMINOES
G 59 WOOD. Double six set made from selected hardwood, polished black with white spots.
G 60 RAINBOW. As G 59 but with a different coloured spot for each number.

BEETLE GAME G 69

SNAKES AND LADDERS G 38

LOTTO G 124

CHAD VALLEY

A page from the Chad Valley centenary catalogue, published in 1960. Chad Valley's connection with Harborne began in 1897, when Johnson Bros. (Stationers and Printers) diversified into toys and moved into a newly built factory on Rose Road. The firm later expanded into the old Harborne Institute on Station Road and the Wee-Kin Works on Park Hill Road.

The directors' office at Chad Valley, *c.* 1900, commanding a view of operations not unlike that from the captain's bridge. The firm's great days were to come between the wars, when there was little competition from imported toys. Jigsaws were all hand made, and helped win the company a royal warrant in 1938.

Office staff at Chad Valley, *c.* 1900. The firm proved responsive to social and cultural change, being the first toy company to jump on the Disney promotional bandwagon, and later exploiting the popularity of television characters like Sooty and Muffin the Mule.

Chad Valley staff group in the late 1920s. In spite of the Johnson Bros. celebrating their centenary in 1960, a series of take-overs ended in the closure of the Harborne factory in 1972. The buildings were subsequently demolished; but the firm's name survives in Chad Valley Close, whose flats now occupy the site.

The interior of Harborne Library in 1910. Formerly the local Masonic Hall, it was opened in 1892 following adaptations costing £2,567.

Harborne Library staff in 1939.

Story hour at Harborne Library, 1976.

Donald Wright (1918-77), seen here in the 1950s when in charge of the old Commercial Library on Great Charles Street, spent his whole career with Birmingham Library Services, including several years at Harborne Library. He worked mainly in Birmingham Central Library, ultimately becoming Head of Reference Services. He was well known as an authority on the history of Harborne, both as writer and lecturer, and bequeathed a large local history archive to Harborne Library. This consisted of photographs both collected and taken by himself, as well as numerous boxes of ephemeral material. Many of the photographs in this book were drawn from his collection.

The first horse bus ran between Harborne and Birmingham, c. 1840, taking an hour, but becoming an instant success, since it also catered for people travelling for short distances. Initially, dozens appeared, mostly operated by proprietors owning one or two vehicles only; but by 1849 the service was run solely by a Mr Turner, who ultimately amalgamated with a later rival, Mr Taylor. This photograph of c. 1900 shows a bus owned by City of Birmingham Tramways, licensed at this time to operate nine horse buses per hour between New Street and Harborne.

This Thornycroft motor bus, also operated by City of Birmingham Tramways, was actually hired from London Motor Omnibus Co., and was run in Birmingham for a few months during 1905. It is seen here at Five Ways on the Birmingham-Harborne run. With a rear entrance and outside stairs, it carried twelve passengers inside and eighteen upstairs.

Built in 1912 for Midland Red (successor of CBT), this Tilling-Stevens motor bus was taken over in October 1914 by Birmingham Corporation following the city's Act of the same year; thirty buses were transferred along with the Tennant Street (Five Ways) garage. Seen here, in around 1920, and withdrawn in 1924, it carried sixteen passengers inside and eighteen outside. There was a rear entrance and external staircase.

A motor bus bound for Birmingham, with solid tyres and outside stairs, waits by Harborne Terrace, c. 1926. Although the possibility of a tram service to Harborne had been considered, plans were abandoned following opposition from the Calthorpe Estate, who allowed tram services on the fringes of Edgbaston (Hagley Road and Bristol Road), but vetoed trams passing through Chad Valley, the heart of the garden suburb.

A Tilling-Stevens motor bus, also bound for Birmingham, waits by Harborne Terrace in the early 1920s. These 40hp buses had a petrol-electric transmission, by which a petrol engine drove an electric motor, which then drove the propeller shaft to provide power to the back wheels.

Steam roller in the High Street, c. 1920.

The Outer Circle Bus Route, one of the longest in Britain completely within the bounds of a city, was established in 1926, traversing new territory while also linking together some existing services. The circular route was originally intended for tramcars; but parts were in essence still country lanes and proved inadequate. Suitably upgraded where appropriate, however, the existing roads were usable by buses. The twenty-five mile long route took just over two hours; the total journey cost 1s 3d (6p) at the time of opening. This illustration forms the cover of a 1932 Guide to the route, which was for some years a popular tourist attraction. Harborne figured prominently in the itinerary, its newly widened roads being singled out for particular praise. Lordswood Road had been 'converted in recent years from a country lane into a magnificent thoroughfare', while Harborne Park Road's widening had been 'carried out on the best lines, and little of the former picturesqueness has been lost'.

Harborne Railway Station, c. 1930. Opposition from affected landowners led to the abandonment of the original plan for a Birmingham-Halesowen Railway, and the stretch to Harborne from Monument Lane, on the Wolverhampton main line, was all that was ever built. A single-track line was finally opened on 10 August 1874. Although an independent firm, the Harborne Railway Company had an arrangement with the LNWR whereby the latter ran the line with its own staff and stock in return for 50% of the gross receipts.

Harborne Station staff in the 1920s. In its heyday, the line was profitable, running twenty-seven trains each way per day in 1914 on a fifteen-minute journey, according to a contemporary timetable. After the First World War however serious competition was being felt from motor buses, whose route was shorter and more direct than the railway. Serious delays were frequently encountered at the Monument Lane mainline junction, making nonsense of the timetable, and the slowness of the Harborne Railway became latterly something of a music-hall joke.

Harborne Station in 1950. Passenger services had ceased as early as 24 November 1934 (at which time the return third class fare to Birmingham was 3d, i.e., 1p). Goods services, however, continued to operate until 1963, there being several major customers, including the M & B Brewery at Cape Hill and Chad Valley Toys. In the picture, the Chad Valley factory can be seen behind the station buildings.

On 3 June 1950, the Stephenson Locomotive Society ran a special train (seen here, with ex-LN-WR tank 46757) from Birmingham New Street to Harborne. The final train to visit Harborne Station – also an S.L.S. special – ran on 2 November 1963.

The abandoned railway rapidly 'returned to nature', as can be seen in this view of a cutting in 1975.

Following closure, various proposals were considered for the track bed, including conversion to a relief road; but finally the City Council agreed to purchase the land from British Rail for £15,000 and convert it to a walkway. Restoration work is seen here in progress in the summer of 1981. The public walkway was formally opened on 6 November of that year by Sir Richard Marsh, himself a former chairman of BR.

Harborne Volunteer Fire Brigade, c. 1890. Founded in 1879 by Charles Hart of Harborne Hall (who was also its first captain), it benefited from a public appeal of 1881, which yielded £190 for the provision of an engine, accessories and uniform, and fitted out premises in Serpentine Road as a fire station. By 1883 the brigade was dealing with seven fires a year, in each case getting the engine or hose cart horsed within five minutes of the alarm.

The Volunteer Fire Brigade, again c. 1890. In 1884 the brigade received official recognition from Harborne Local Board, who thereafter helped financially with the maintenance of their fire appliances. By 1889 electric alarm bells were installed at the fire station and other premises, and in addition a number of hand bells were sited at strategic points around the village. One bell was rung on sighting the fire, then another, then another, in chain reaction. In 1891, when Harborne was taken into Birmingham, the Volunteers were disbanded and replaced by full-time members of the Birmingham Fire Brigade.

Tonks' Garage, on Harborne High Street, in the late 1930s. Albert Tonks, who had previously run a garage on Monument Road, had expanded into Harborne by 1925. The garage survived into the late 1980s, the site now being occupied by Lingfield Court flats.

Five

Institutions

St Peter's church and the Old Vicarage in the 1930s.

St Peter's church, from an engraving of c. 1820. Although an older church had probably previously occupied the site, the first documentary evidence is for 1217. The present (much reconstructed) building was probably started in the early thirteenth century, and completed towards
the end of the fourteenth; the Black Death could well have delayed operations. The registers date
back to 1538, and are thus almost contemporary with Thomas Cromwell's edict of 5 September
of that year that every parish should keep records of baptisms, marriages and burials. The first
entry is for the burial of Henri Carles – possibly the wood-man of Carles Wood, which later gave
its name to Carless Avenue. Thomas Wood's 'golden cockerel' weather vane of 1774 can be
clearly seen in the picture, as can the gables of the present Bell Inn to the right of the tower.

St Peter's church, *c.* 1900. Although ivy-clad, it appears in its recognisably modern form following the partial rebuilding of 1867, supervised by the vicar, the Revd Edward Roberts. The architect was Yeoville Thomason (who also designed Birmingham Council House), and by retaining both the tower and much of the medieval north wall, he was able to complete the rebuilding for £3,500.

The interior of St Peter's, also around 1900, showing the galleries which formerly occupied three sides of the church. In 1928, however, at the wedding of the very popular Dr Morton, the congregation was so large that the galleries began to creak alarmingly, and – apart from those in the two transepts – they were soon afterwards taken down.

The grave of the artist David Cox (1783-1859), seen here in the 1930s, is to be found in St Peter's churchyard, not far beyond the east end of the church, which also contains a memorial window to him. Born in Deritend, Birmingham, he moved to London at the age of twenty-one, earning his living by teaching and painting, being himself largely self-taught. In 1841, he gave up teaching and returned to Birmingham, settling at Greenfield House in Greenfield Road, at this time still a country lane. Some of his landscape paintings are said to have been inspired directly by the local scenery. His oil painting of St Peter's church (which he attended) is in Dublin Art Gallery, and there is a watercolour of the Old Vicarage in Birmingham Art Gallery.

James Thomas Law (1790-1876) was Vicar of St Peter's from 1825 to 1845, as well as being Chancellor of the Diocese of Lichfield and Honorary Warden of the Birmingham School of Medicine. The author of numerous works on theology and church law, he was also popular with parishioners, having the common touch and taking a cut in tithe payments at a time of agricultural depression. He rejuvenated the parish following years of neglect, and supervised the first partial rebuilding of the church. He built a new vicarage, and a new house for his curate. He also established what is now St Peter's school on its present site, merging the existing National schools opposite the church with the old Free school from the High Street.

Edward Roberts (1819-91) was curate at St Peter's from 1853 to 1858, and then vicar till 1891. Known as 'Moses' because of his large bushy beard, he was a homely preacher and excelled as a pastor. During his ministry, the church was enlarged and substantially rebuilt, so that to-day only the tower survives virtually intact. His wife Elizabeth ran a school at the vicarage throughout his ministry, and following her death in 1890 a lychgate was erected by her former pupils in her memory.

Pupils at the Vicarage school, *c.* 1890, with Mrs Roberts standing in the back row, in front of the door. She had started her first school at Kingswood, near Bristol, when her husband was curate there, and the school in Harborne became so popular that a special schoolroom was erected.

St Peter's school, c. 1900. James Thomas Law, when Vicar of Harborne, organised the construction of the National schools opposite the church, c. 1837. The schoolmaster's cottage from that date is therefore the oldest building in Birmingham still used as a school. The vicar later arranged for the merger of this school with the old Free school in the High Street, founded in 1707 and rebuilt in 1821. There were originally two schoolrooms and a teacher's house; a schoolroom was added in 1848, and there were further enlargements in 1872.

St Peter's school, c. 1907, following further alterations. The school was further extended in 1912, and became a controlled school in 1953. By 1961 it had thirteen classrooms.

A classroom at St Peter's in 1929.

Red Cross cadets at St Peter's in the 1960s – one of several uniformed organisations associated with the church. The world's first Girl Guides came from Harborne, the first Harborne troop being authorised by Lady Baden Powell, following the attendance of thirteen local girls at Warley Woods scout rally in 1909.

St Mary's Catholic church, Vivian Road, c. 1910. Following a request by Bishop Ullathorne, the Passionist Order sent a community of priests to his Birmingham diocese, setting up Harborne's first Roman Catholic church in the former Methodist chapel on the High Street in 1870. They opened a school the following year, and remained there till 1873, when they heard that Harborne Lodge, on what was then Lodge Road, was for sale. They bought the Lodge, and started to hold services there immediately, while a new church was being built in the grounds

St Mary's church and school in 1995. The church was completed on its new Lodge Road (later Vivian Road) site in 1877, but was not consecrated until 1932, when all debts had been paid. The old Methodist chapel on the High Street served solely as a school until 1895, when new school buildings were provided on Vivian Road, alongside the church. There were two class-rooms for 109 pupils. The school was enlarged in 1937, in 1954, and again in 1963. Aided status came in 1953.

St Mary's school group in 1900, with Miss Nene, Father Russell and Miss Lane.

St Mary's school class in 1905, with Miss Nolan and Mrs Donnelly. Miss Nolan was headmistress from 1899 to 1926.

Country dancing at St Mary's in 1926.

St Mary's school class in 1930, with Miss Seely.

St Faith's Mission church choir, c. 1910. In 1906, St Peter's parish had built St Faith's Mission in Court Oak Road to serve the northern part of the parish. The neighbouring parish of Christ Church, Quinton, had built St Lawrence's Mission in Aubrey Road in 1901.

The two missions were combined in 1933 into the new parish of St Faith and St Lawrence. Philip Chatwin's new church on Court Oak Road was consecrated in 1937. Between 1958 and 1960 a chancel, sanctuary, Lady Chapel and vestries were added by Philip Chatwin and his nephew Anthony. This brick-built church is of a harmonious Arts and Crafts design, with a Romanesque arcaded interior partly whitened and partly of plain brick. The church, as seen here in 1964, stands on the site of the original St Faith's Mission Hall of corrugated iron.

Harborne Baptist church, on the High Street, c. 1920. A Baptist mission had been present in Harborne since 1787, the Baptists meeting from 1820 in a private house, and subsequently at the Fish Inn, North Road. In 1836, the first chapel was purchased from the Congregationalists for £350. A purpose-built chapel was erected in 1864-5 and enlarged in 1877, 1901 and 1926.

Demolition of the old Baptist church in 1971. It was replaced by a new purpose-built church in Harborne Park Road, and the old site redeveloped as offices (later converted to apartments and ground floor shops).

South Street Methodist church in the 1970s. Methodist preachers began to visit Harborne in 1837, at first renting a room behind the Fish Inn for their services. A purpose-built chapel was erected on the High Street in 1839; this building still survives behind modern shop extensions. In 1868, the Methodists moved to a larger chapel in South Street; seating 500 and costing £2,500, it was designed by Martin and Chamberlain. The South Street premises were extended in 1875,1888 and 1895. By 1940 there were eleven ancillary rooms, including a school hall. At least three of the ministers have become president of the Methodist Conference.

Salvation Army wedding, c. 1945. The Salvation Army were first established in Harborne High Street in 1915, remaining there till the late 1990s, when they moved to Lonsdale Road. Marks and Spencer now occupy the site.

Once a junior school, the Clock Tower Adult Education Centre, on the High Street, is seen here in the 1980s. Known initially as Harborne Heath Road Board school, it was designed by Martin and Chamberlain and opened in 1881 as a mixed school; an infants'department was then added, the accommodation being for 398, with a teacher's house. The infants were transferred to Station Road in 1912, and the school was altered and reorganised as a junior mixed in 1931. By 1955 there were ten classrooms.

Diamond Jubilee commemoration at Harborne High Street Board school, as it was known from 1883. It later became the High Street County Primary school. Following its later role as an adult education centre, the building is now a mixed residential and restaurant complex.

Group of High Street Board school children, chosen to go on to secondary school, in 1935.

Station Road Infants' Class, c. 1934. Originally opened as Station Road Board school in 1902, the school, which included a teacher's house, accommodated 336 boys. In 1912, the premises were enlarged to accommodate 500, including the infants from the High Street school. The building was altered and enlarged in 1928, and reorganised for senior mixed and infants in 1931.

Station Road school football team, 1939. From 1945 to 1957, the senior department operated separately in an adjoining building, which was later used by the High Street school. The two sites were subsequently run as a single primary school.

Harborne Hall, seen from the lake in its extensive wooded grounds. It was at this time, (c. 1921), a preparatory school run by Montagu Lawson, previously of West House school, Edgbaston. The school lasted from 1919 to 1924.

Harborne Hall school farm, with St Peter's church in the background, *c.* 1921. The farm supplied dairy produce; and the school also encouraged gardening and nature study. Each boy had his own garden, and botany was taught in the gardens. The school had its own natural history museum.

A riding class at Harborne Hall school, *c.* 1921. Sports offered included cricket, football, tennis, golf, swimming, paper chases, shooting and boxing, all taught by specialists. The practical and the aesthetic were equally emphasised, with carpentry, drawing, music and photography all regularly taught.

P.E. class at Harborne Hall school, *c.* 1921. The boys were drilled in deep breathing and put through essential exercises each morning. The galleried reception hall was used for dancing classes in the winter. Country walking was also encouraged.

Formerly a private house, Baskerville House, on Court Oak Road, was used for some years as a school for the physically handicapped. Now demolished, it is seen here in around 1920.

Lordswood Boys' school, seen soon after completion in 1957, was at this time a grammar technical school; its streamlined, confident architectural style seemed to embody the progressive optimism of post war education.

The entrance hall at Lordswood Boys' school, also c. 1957, with the pupils literally walking towards the light – another publicity photograph for the new school. Lordswood Boys' became a comprehensive in 1973. From 1983 it shared its sixth form with the neighbouring Lordswood Girls' School; but since 1996 the two schools have organised separate sixth form provision. Pupils come today from a wide range of backgrounds – from parts of Edgbaston, Winson Green and Ladywood, as well as Harborne.

The Kindergarten school for Blind Children, Court Oak Road, *c.* 1910. Founded in 1903 as a junior branch of the then Royal Institution for the Blind in Edgbaston, Queen Alexandra College (as it is now known) has today succeeded Edgbaston in its all-round provision of education for the blind in Birmingham, offering two-year vocational courses which place an emphasis on living skills, orientation and mobility as well as work experience. There are special facilities for learning office skills (including ICT and telecommunications), machine tool engineering and cycle mechanics. Music (whether for work or leisure) features prominently.

Six

Leisure and Sport

Old Church Avenue, *c.* 1905, runs between the cricket fields towards St Peter's church.

Harborne Cricket Ground, beside Old Church Avenue, c. 1907. In 1868, both St Peter's and the Baptist church had flourishing youth clubs, and on 4 May of that year a meeting of young men from both clubs was held in the Baptist Hall, to form a cricket club. Matches were held initially in a field off Richmond Hill Road; but in 1874 the club leased the present ground, where it has since remained. Harborne Hockey Club, using the same ground in winter, was formed in 1903.

Harborne Cricket Club players, 1880.

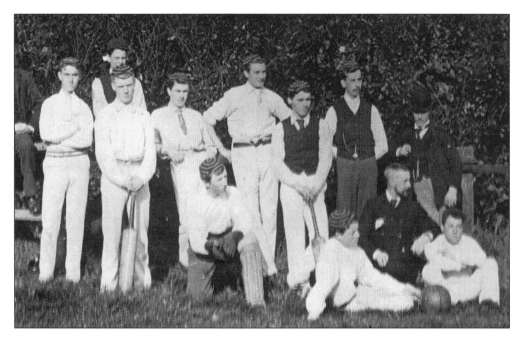

The 1905 Cricket Club team.

Harborne Ladies' Cricket Club, at the time of their match with the men's cricket team in 1912. When playing against them, the men bowled and batted left-handed.

Sports day on the cricket field, *c.* 1930.

Spectators at a Harborne cricket club match in 1964.

St Peter's Young People's Society Football Club, 1938.

Harborne Golf Club was founded on 14 October 1893, following a meeting at the Harborne and Edgbaston Institute, the moving spirits being George Hart and Arthur Godlee. Land on both sides of Northfield Road (Church Farm and Home Farm) was laid out initially as two nine-hole courses. Church Farm tithe barn on Vicarage Road was converted into a clubhouse, and used till 1905, when it was replaced by the present Tennal Road building, seen here in 1966. By 1902 a single eighteen-hole course was ready.

At the first tee of Church Farm Golf Course in 1927. Originally part of Harborne Golf Course, it was acquired by Birmingham Corporation in October 1924, and opened in 1926 as a separate nine-hole municipal course. Harborne Golf Club, meanwhile, converted their Home Farm site into a full-scale eighteen-hole course.

The view across Church Farm Golf Course towards Vicarage Road in 1973. The clubhouse, seen to the right, stands on the site of the former tithe barn used by Harborne Golf Club as their first clubhouse. Just beyond this, a retaining wall made of old retorts marks the spot where a road once began to cross the former farmland. The club handbook stated in 1927: 'The combination of natural and artificial hazards with well bunkered greens gives the course a sporting nature'.

Yachting on Harborne Reservoir in 1950. The Worcester and Birmingham Canal (constructed under Act of Parliament 1790/1) crossed the line of the River Rea and its tributary the Bourn Brook, and to ensure that mill owners using river water still had sufficient left to drive their machinery, the canal proprietors were obliged to construct and maintain this reservoir in compensation.

By the mid-twentieth century, local mills were no longer using water power, and the reservoir served no purpose for the canal, being at a lower level. Following an Act of 1958, it was decided to drain the reservoir and find an alternative use for the site. By 1972, the reservoir had been partially filled in for housing, while the remaining area had been converted into open space, as seen in this 1977 view of the breached retaining wall and embankment. A footpath now traverses the partly wooded site, linking Harborne Lane and Northfield Road, and beyond that the 'greenway' through Clapgate Lane and Woodgate Valley.

Moorpool Tennis Courts, *c.* 1909, formed from the beginning one of the recreational facilities of the Moorpool Estate. They are still well used today.

The Moorpool Bowling Club, situated in sylvan surroundings beside the Moor Pool, is another long-standing sporting facility, seen here in around 1960.

The Moor Pool, fed by a spring and a natural focal point of the Moorpool Estate, is shown here, again in around 1960, with the bowling pavilion on the bank and estate housing glimpsed through the trees beyond.

Cleaning the Moor Pool in the 1960s.

Fishing in the Moor Pool in the 1970s.

Waiting for the No.11 opposite Harborne Swimming Baths in 1966, with summer theatre at Cannon Hill Park prominently advertised by the roadside. The baths, consisting of a swimming bath and twenty-three private baths, were opened on 13 December 1928. A brand new building, offering both swimming and gymnastic facilities, was recently opened on the site.

Queen's Park, seen here c. 1905, was bought by public subscription to celebrate Queen Victoria's Diamond Jubilee, and opened by the Lord Mayor on 5 October 1898. There was formerly a bandstand, and the Harborne Carnival was at one time held regularly here.

Queen's Park, c. 1913. It was stipulated, at the time of laying out the park, that there should be adequate playing facilities for children. The adjacent road, Turks Lane, was renamed Queen's Park Road at the same time.

A Baptist church Sunday morning study group of amateur gardeners visiting The Grove in the 1930s.

The Grove Park in winter, looking towards Harborne Park Road, in the 1960s.

Grove Park in the summer of 1974. The park formerly contained other pools, now filled in, including Tinker's Pool, where a copse now flourishes. The huge cedar tree just off the picture forms part of the original eighteenth-century garden (the house, Victorian on earlier foundations, having been demolished in 1963). Remains of medieval ridge and furrow ploughing may still be seen in the large playing field to the right of the picture.

Summer in Grove Park in 1974, showing part of the railed driveway to the now demolished house, and an attractive summerhouse (also now demolished).

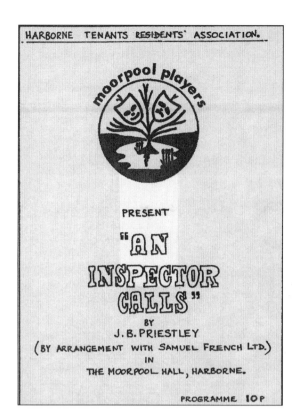

The Queen's Silver Jubilee celebrations of 1977 led to the formation of the Harborne Tenants Residents' Association, and thence to the idea of staging amateur theatre at the Moorpool Hall. The Moorpool Players' first production was Noel Coward's *Blithe Spirit* (1978), which was a great success, in spite of some technical problems. Their first real drama was J.B. Priestley's *An Inspector Calls* (1981).

An Inspector Calls (pictured here) led to performances of other serious modern drama, including *The Diary of Anne Frank* and *Anastasia* (both 1984), Terence Rattigan's *The Deep Blue Sea* (1989) and Daphne du Maurier's *Rebecca* (1990). In 1990, *The Deep Blue Sea* received the Philip Rodway award for serious drama.

110

Willy Russell's *Educating Rita* (1998) was one of several notable comedy productions. Others have included J.B. Priestley's *When we are Married* (1986), Noel Coward's *Hay Fever* (1988), Alan Ayckbourn's *Confusions* (1991), and Mike Leigh's *Abigail's Party* (1992).

THE MOORPOOL PLAYERS
Affiliated to NODA

present

EDUCATING RITA

by Willy Russell

Tuesday 28th April to
Saturday 2nd May 1998

7.30pm at Moorpool Hall,
The Circle, Harborne

Educating Rita (pictured here, starring John Healey and Carey Hardy), is an instance of the Players' willingness to tackle the bigger and more challenging roles, as was their production in the same year of Willy Russell's *Shirley Valentine*, a monumental monologue performance. The Players have received professional help for some individual productions, and several sponsored performances have taken place at other theatres.

111

The original Old House at Home, on Lordswood Road, was situated about 300 yards up the road from the present pub (which was built to serve the extensive new inter-war housing developments in the area). Probably dating from the seventeenth century, the old pub at this time (c. 1900) stood on what was virtually a country lane, its simple domestic style appropriate in a still semi-rural area of scattered cottages and working farms.

The Court Oak, Balden Road, was designed by George Bernard Cox, and is shown here not long after completion in 1932. In the Spanish *hacienda* style, with green roof tiling and white-painted brickwork, it was a new licence aimed at the major new housing estates planned for the area. The pub has two striking three-dimensional signs, one free-standing, and one fixed over the central entrance door. At the rear is an extensive formal walled garden with loggias-an important feature in 'reformed' pubs of this type, which aimed to provide facilities for the whole family.

The Duke of York, in 1963, for long a well-known bus stage, stood at the junction of Lordswood Road and Harborne High Street. A late Victorian pub built on the site of an older building, it contained a large assembly room once the venue for frequent musical events. It was recently demolished, and the site is now occupied by retirement flats.

The King's Arms in the 1980s, seen from Albert Walk. The pub was rebuilt in the 1930s, replacing a late Victorian pub which had itself replaced a much older building, probably of seventeenth-century origin. The original King's Arms at one time offered bull baiting as an entertainment, and was the scene in 1812 of the founding of the Harborne Friendly Society, which provided a private insurance scheme long before the days of state benefits. Said to have been haunted by the ghost of a young boy who once lived there, the pub was destroyed by a fire in 2013.

The Bell, on Old Church Road, in 1974. In common with many country inns, Harborne's oldest pub was originally a farmhouse (like the Cock at Rubery), and probably began by serving food and drink while still operating as a working farm. Of seventeenth-century origin, with later additions, it stands next to St Peter's church, its beer garden and bowling green overlooked by the churchyard trees and fourteenth-century tower. At one time, it is said to have been a 'Church House', where the Parish Clerk used to supply ale and food to those worshippers who had travelled some distance to the service. The pub cellars are reputed to contain a priest's hole, and many traditional features survive, including a bar passage, serving hatch, ingle-nook fireplace, and original oak beams.

The Golden Cross, at the junction of Harborne Park Road and Metchley Lane, in 1924. This late Victorian pub was soon afterwards replaced by a more modern building, which was in the 1980s renamed the Lazy Fox and more recently the Florence and Firkin. The pub was recently demolished, and the site is now occupied by student flats.

The rear yard of the Vine, on the High Street, in 1966. The original Vine Inn, of eighteenth-century origin, still retained something of the air of a coaching inn, with its long range of outbuildings reached through a massive doorway from the street, and its large 'outdoor' drinking area, giving access to several small rooms. It was refurbished in the late 1970s, and finally replaced in 1989 by a completely new pub of a 'modern-traditional' style.

The New Inn, Vivian Road, in 1964. Of eighteenth-century origin, the New Inn probably began as a private residence, as this 'unimproved' view suggests. In recent years, some of the outbuildings at the rear have been demolished and the interior successfully refurbished. The public bar retains a fine Victorian bar-back. Like several Harborne pubs, the New Inn has a well-used beer garden.

The Sportsman, Metchley Lane, c. 1960, is another cottage-style pub like the White Horse; both pubs may have started as private houses, in contrast to the later purpose-built gin palaces or inter-war roadhouses. The comedienne Victoria Wood worked here while studying at Birmingham University. The pub has a large beer garden, and – as befits its name–its own cricket team. Like its near neighbour, the Green Man, it was once the venue for gooseberry growing contests.

Looking from the High Street towards Edgbaston in 1939, with the Plough Inn on the left and the original Green Man on the right; rows of nail makers' cottages extend beyond the pillar box. A private house in the eighteenth century, the Plough was a coaching inn by the 1840s. The Green Man, soon to be replaced by the present pub, dated from the early nineteenth century, and was noted at one time for its fine strawberry gardens, and also as the home of the Gooseberry Growers' Society, founded in 1815 and producing the country's largest gooseberry in 1875.

The Green Man, c. 1965, with the Blue Coat school in the background. Standing beside the Harborne / Edgbaston boundary (which runs down Metchley Lane), the present pub was built in around 1939 in a harmonious Arts and Crafts style, with a prominent corner sign depicting the Green Man as a huntsman rather than a nature spirit. Reconstructed internally on several occasions – currently with a large island bar and various inter-linked rooms – the Green Man is notable for its large number of sports teams, and enjoys a well-used bowling green.

Snow games at St Peter's Vicarage school in the winter of 1888/89.

The Vicarage school snow house, 1888/89.

Seven

Events

St Peter's Vicarage school outing, *c.* 1885.

Mrs Neville Chamberlain laying the foundation stone of St Peter's Parish Hall on 3 October 1953, in the presence of the Revd Sidney Harvie Clark, vicar from 1947 to 1967. In a simple but dignified speech, Mrs Chamberlain recalled her earlier launching of a ship, and adapted her blessing to this occasion: 'May God bless this hall and guard and keep all who enter into its fellowship'. The hall was subsequently opened on 30 June 1954 by the Bishop of Birmingham, Dr J.L. Wilson. Born Anne Vere Cole, Mrs Chamberlain married Neville Chamberlain in 1911, and until his death in 1941 tirelessly supported him in his various roles as Birmingham councillor, Lord Mayor, M.P., and ultimately Prime Minister. Active herself in Conservative women's circles and as a political hostess, she died in 1967 at the age of eighty-four and is buried in St Peter's churchyard.

St Peter's church outing, *c.* 1900.

Nativity play at St Peter's in the 1950s.

Vicarage fête at St Peter's in the 1930s.

St Peter's Young People's Society Dance at Moorpool Hall, 12 May 1939.

A performance of *Comus* was given for the summer pageant at St Mary's school in 1926.

St Mary's school celebrated their centenary (1995) in a variety of ways, including the presentation of a souvenir mug to each child at a ceremony in the assembly hall.

May Day festivities at the Moorpool Estate in 1909. As at Bournville, such traditional celebrations were felt to be appropriate in a closely-knit 'village' community.

May Day festivities, Moorpool Estate, 1909.

HARBORNE TENANTS' MAY-DAY FESTIVITIES, 14th MAY, 1910.

Moorpool festivities, 14 May 1910.

Coronation celebrations (1953) in the Moorpool Hall.

As a conscious heir of Victorian 'record' photographers like Sir Benjamin Stone, Donald Wright made it his business to record the changing face of Harborne–not only through street scenes and individual buildings, but also in the recording of significant local events. Harborne Carnival, held variously over the years in Queen's Park, the Cricket Ground, and Harborne High Street, has for long been prominent on the local calendar as a charitable fund-raising festival. The 1969 Carnival was held on the Cricket Ground.

Stands at the 1969 Harborne Carnival. Prominent among these is that of the Harborne Society, founded in 1960, which is concerned with conserving the essential character of Harborne and fostering a strong community spirit.

A gymnastic display, at the 1969 Carnival.

Scottish dancing at the Carnival, again in 1969.

The last match of the centenary year of Harborne Cricket Club, September 1968.